MW00951954

# LUCID DREAMING

## A BEGINNER'S GUIDE TO MASTERING YOUR DREAMS

ALISON REED

# CONTENTS

# INTRODUCTION

Welcome to "Lucid Dreaming: A Beginner's Guide to Mastering Your Dreams," a comprehensive journey into the fascinating world of lucid dreaming. This book is designed for those who are curious about exploring the limitless landscapes of their subconscious mind while they sleep. Whether you are a complete novice to the concept of lucid dreaming or someone with a bit of experience looking to deepen your practice, this guide is crafted to take you step by step through the process of not only understanding what lucid dreaming is but also how you can begin to experience it for yourself.

Our journey begins with "Understanding Sleep," where we delve into the mechanics of sleep and its various phases. It's essential to grasp how sleep works to appreciate the stages where lucid dreaming becomes possible. From there, we venture into the realm of dreams with "Why Do We Dream?" exploring the theories behind why our brains conjure these nightly visions and the potential benefits they hold.

Equipped with a foundational understanding of sleep and dreams, "How to Lucid Dream" introduces you to the initial techniques and practices that can open the door to conscious dreaming. You'll learn about reality checks and other strategies that can help trigger lucidity, setting the stage for an adventure like no other.

Lucid dreaming is not just an intriguing phenomenon; it offers a host of "Lucid Dreaming Benefits," which we explore in depth. From creative problem-solving and overcoming nightmares to enhancing your waking life through the insights gained in your dreams, the advantages of lucid dreaming are vast and varied.

"Exploring the Dream World" encourages you to dive deeper into your lucid dreams, offering guidance on how to interact with dream characters, alter your environment, and even control the narrative of your dreams. This chapter opens up a playground for your mind, where the only limit is your imagination.

For those ready to take their practice to the next level, "Advanced Techniques" introduces more sophisticated methods of dream control and exploration. These techniques are designed to refine your ability to induce lucid dreams and enhance the clarity and stability of your dream experiences.

"Lucid Dreaming: A Beginner's Guide to Mastering Your Dreams" is more than just a book; it's an invitation to embark on a transformative journey that bridges the gap between the conscious and subconscious mind. As you turn each page, you'll be equipped with the knowledge and tools needed to unlock the full potential of your dream world, opening up a universe of possibilities for personal growth, creativity, and self-discovery. Welcome to the beginning of your lucid dreaming adventure.

# CHAPTER 1:
# UNDERSTANDING SLEEP

Sleep is an essential aspect of life, serving as a crucial time for rejuvenation, healing, and rest, vital for all living beings. Yet, in today's fast-paced world, sleep is often relegated to a secondary status, viewed more as a luxury than a necessity. Amidst the hustle and bustle, many people treat sleep as a last resort, only succumbing to it when absolutely necessary, aiming to get just enough rest to fuel another day's activities. This trend is alarmingly widespread, with a significant portion of the population squeezed into such patterns by the demanding pressures of work, academic pursuits, or family obligations.

Society's relentless pace has made it increasingly challenging to prioritize sleep, a stark contrast to the natural world, where sleep forms the cornerstone of most animals' existence. Unlike them, humans juggle the additional burden of financial responsibilities, making us uniquely prone to sacrificing sleep on an unprecedented scale. The irony is that despite sleep's critical role in both physical and mental well-being, and its indirect contribution to success, it often falls to the bottom of people's priority lists. In an ironic twist, individuals aiming for success might forgo adequate rest, opting instead for an early morning workout, under the mistaken belief that this compensates for the lack of sleep. However, no amount of physical activity, balanced diet, hydration, or hygiene can substitute for the loss of sleep. Many overlook sleep's profound healing properties, viewing it merely as a means to recharge energy, rather than recognizing it as a potent, albeit slow-acting, remedy for numerous health issues. While sleep may not cure every ailment on its own, its absence almost invariably exacerbates health problems. Sleep is a remarkable, effortless tool that requires nothing more than closing our eyes and allowing ourselves to detach from the conscious world.

The advantages of sufficient sleep are nearly boundless. It's commonly accepted that an average of eight hours of sleep per night is optimal for a healthy and fulfilling lifestyle. Yet, this standard often serves more as an aspirational target than a goal actively pursued by the majority. In the United States, a staggering 35.2% of adults regularly fail to achieve adequate sleep. This group can generally be divided into two segments: those overwhelmed by the demands of life, leaving scant time for rest, and those who deliberately delay bedtime in favor of other activities. While it's tempting to attribute the sleep deficit of the latter to personal choice, the situation is far from simple.

Numerous factors beyond work, school, and daily chores impact an individual's sleep patterns. A significant obstacle is the scarcity of time for leisure activities post-work. Many individuals return home from a long day only to spend their evenings engrossed in movies, hobbies, or socializing, sacrificing sleep in the process. Though this reflects a deliberate decision, it's also a deeply relatable one given the finite nature of our days.

Adequate sleep is critical for a host of physiological benefits affecting every system and organ in the body. Notably, it significantly bolsters the immune system, our body's defense mechanism against disease and illness. This system relies on a suite of specialized molecules and cells to ward off infections. Sleep prompts the immune system to produce cytokines, small proteins that enhance the functioning of immune and blood cells. Among these are T cells, key players in identifying and neutralizing foreign pathogens by activating B cells to generate necessary antibodies. Insufficient sleep disrupts the production of T cells, diminishing the body's immune response and heightening the risk of illness and allergies.

Sleep significantly influences our weight management by directly affecting hormones that regulate hunger and satiety. Specifically, adequate sleep balances the levels of ghrelin, the hormone that signals hunger, and leptin, which signals fullness. When sleep is insufficient, ghrelin levels rise, increasing our appetite, while leptin levels drop, making it harder to feel satiated. This imbalance often leads to overeating and a preference for high-calorie, energy-dense foods and beverages, particularly those rich in caffeine, to counteract feelings of lethargy. Consequently, this pattern can elevate the risk of obesity and related health issues over time due to the excess caloric intake beyond what the body needs for a healthy lifestyle.

Moreover, sleep's role extends to cardiovascular health by modulating stress-related hormones. Inadequate sleep triggers an increase in cortisol, a stress hormone that demands more effort from the heart, potentially leading to hypertension, cardiovascular disease, type 2 diabetes, and even heart attacks. This overexertion of the heart due to heightened cortisol levels underscores the necessity of sufficient sleep for maintaining heart health and preventing long-term damage.

The brain also relies on adequate sleep for emotional and psychological well-being. Short sleep durations are closely linked to a higher risk of mental health disorders, including depression, anxiety, and bipolar disorder. Even outside these conditions, insufficient sleep can escalate daily stress levels and feelings of anxiety, making individuals more reactive to life's challenges. The resulting fatigue impairs cognitive functions, such as attention and memory, diminishing productivity and the ability to manage tasks effectively.

Intriguingly, a small fraction of the population, estimated at around 5%, operates well on less than six hours of sleep, attributed to a mutation in the DEC2 gene. This genetic variance allows them to enjoy the full benefits of sleep within a significantly condensed period, enabling late nights and early mornings without the typical repercussions of sleep deprivation.

Conversely, many people suffer from sleep disorders like insomnia and sleep apnea, which affect an estimated 50 to 70 million adults in the United States alone. These conditions can severely disrupt sleep patterns, leading to a cascade of health issues if left untreated. The complexity and diversity of sleep disorders underscore the importance of seeking proper medical advice and treatment to mitigate their impact on health and well-being.

## Improving Sleep

For many individuals struggling with sleep, the root cause isn't a biological disorder, but rather, entrenched habits and lifestyle choices. These often include an overreliance on electronic devices and social media, coupled with evening stress or restlessness. If you find yourself facing these obstacles, consider adopting the following strategies to cultivate better sleep habits:

**Implement a Screen Time Shutdown:** Dedicate a specific timeframe each evening to engage with your favorite digital media without guilt. Once this period concludes, discipline yourself to disconnect from all electronic devices. This practice is crucial because the blue light emitted by screens can disrupt your circadian rhythm and suppress melatonin production, the hormone essential for sleep. By creating a digital curfew, you not only reduce blue light exposure but also signal to your brain that it's time to transition into sleep mode.

**Cultivate a Consistent Sleep Routine:** A common complaint is the lack of sleepiness at one's ideal bedtime, often exacerbated by engaging in stimulating activities too close to bedtime. To counter this, avoid any vigorous exercise or mentally demanding tasks in the hours leading up to sleep. Strive for consistency in your sleep schedule, aiming to go to bed and wake up at the same times daily, including weekends. This regularity trains your body's internal clock to expect sleep at certain times, gradually easing the transition into restfulness.

**Design a Pre-Sleep Wind-Down Ritual:** Allot time before bed to engage in calming activities that help you decompress and ease the mind. Consider practices such as journaling to process the day's events and emotions, sipping on a warm, non-caffeinated beverage like herbal tea, or meditating to clear your mind and relax your body. These activities serve as a buffer zone between the day's stresses and sleep, helping to mitigate the mental clutter that can often invade our thoughts as we attempt to fall asleep. Creating a tranquil environment and routine before bed can significantly improve your ability to fall asleep more quickly and enjoy a deeper, more restorative sleep.

**Create a Comforting Bedroom Environment:** Beyond the pre-sleep routine, ensure your sleeping environment is conducive to rest. This can include investing in a comfortable mattress and pillows, using blackout curtains to keep the room dark, and maintaining a cool, comfortable temperature. Consider also the use of white noise machines or earplugs if noise is a concern, and aromatic diffusers with calming scents like lavender can further enhance the sleep-friendly atmosphere of your bedroom.

**Mindful Eating and Drinking Habits:** Pay attention to your diet and its timing in relation to your sleep schedule. Avoid heavy or large meals within a couple of hours of bedtime, as digestive discomfort can disturb sleep. Likewise, minimize caffeine and alcohol intake late in the day, as both can significantly impact your sleep quality and latency.

Incorporating these expanded strategies into your nightly routine can greatly improve your sleep quality and duration. By addressing the habits that disrupt sleep and establishing a serene bedtime ritual, you're setting the stage for a healthier, more restful night's sleep.

## Sleep Cycles

During sleep, we experience a series of distinct sleep stages, each offering unique experiences and benefits. Typically, an individual will cycle through four to six complete sleep cycles per night, influenced by our innate biological rhythms and brain wave patterns. Some people focus on tracking these sleep cycles instead of merely counting hours to ensure they're getting sufficient rest. The initial cycle of the night is usually the briefest, lasting about 70 to 100 minutes, with subsequent cycles extending to between 90 and 120 minutes. Factors such as age, sleep quality on preceding nights, and alcohol consumption can affect the duration and quality of these sleep stages. The sleep cycle comprises four stages, starting with three phases of non-rapid eye movement (NREM) sleep, and concluding with a phase of rapid eye movement (REM) sleep.

Understanding each sleep stage is crucial for those interested in lucid dreaming. By becoming familiar with the characteristics of each stage, you can pinpoint when dreams are most likely to occur during the night. This knowledge also sheds light on when achieving lucidity in dreams is most feasible, offering insights into the optimal moments for becoming conscious within your dreams.

**Stage 1: NREM1**

The initial phase of the sleep cycle is the non-rapid eye movement stage one, known as NREM1. This stage marks the transition from wakefulness to sleep and occurs as you first start to drift off. While awake and fully alert, our brain is bustling with gamma and beta waves, indicative of high engagement and complex cognitive processing. However, as we enter NREM1, the brain shifts gears, producing alpha and theta waves instead. Alpha waves, often associated with states of calm and relaxation found in meditation, initially dominate the brain's activity, especially in the frontal lobe, indicating a relaxed yet conscious state. As sleep deepens into the latter half of NREM1, theta waves take precedence, characterized by their larger amplitudes and slower frequencies, signaling the brain's progression into a more subdued state. This stage witnesses a decrease in heart rate and breathing, a slight drop in core body temperature, and an increase in muscle relaxation, sometimes accompanied by minor twitches. Typically lasting just five to ten minutes, NREM1 is a brief but essential transition into deeper sleep stages. Individuals roused during NREM1 often feel as though they hadn't fallen asleep at all, highlighting the shallow nature of this initial sleep phase.

## Stage 2: NREM2

Following NREM1, the sleep cycle progresses into the second stage of non-rapid eye movement sleep, NREM2, which ushers in a deeper level of relaxation and disengagement from the waking world. This stage extends for approximately 30 to 60 minutes and is marked by the cessation of eye movements, a further reduction in body temperature, and the stabilization of heart rate and breathing at a more regular pace. During NREM2, the brain continues to produce theta waves, but these are now interspersed with distinctive patterns of brain activity known as sleep spindles and K-complexes. Sleep spindles, brief surges of high-frequency brain waves lasting around a second, play a crucial role in memory consolidation and cognitive processes related to learning. They represent moments when the brain reviews and strengthens new information and skills acquired during the day. K-complexes, in contrast, are singular, high-amplitude waves in the delta frequency range, triggered by external stimuli or sudden changes in the sleep environment. They serve as a bridge to deeper stages of sleep and are thought to protect sleep quality by keeping the sleeper in a tranquil state despite external disruptions. Together, these phenomena underscore NREM2's role in cognitive maintenance and restoration, making it a foundational component of a healthy sleep cycle.

## Stage 3: NREM3

NREM3 marks the transition into deep sleep, also known as slow-wave sleep (SWS), following the lighter sleep stages of NREM1 and NREM2. During NREM3, the brain significantly reduces its activity, primarily emitting delta waves—the slowest and highest-amplitude brain waves, indicative of the deepest levels of relaxation and restorative sleep. Interestingly, techniques like listening to binaural beats before bedtime can encourage the production of delta waves, aiding the transition into deep sleep. In this stage, the sleeper becomes less responsive to external stimuli, making it much more challenging to awaken them. Both the breathing and heart rate decrease substantially, facilitating profound physical relaxation. It's during NREM3 that the body undertakes crucial repair work, healing tissues, and bolstering the immune system. Similarly, the brain consolidates memories and processes information gathered throughout the day, reinforcing learning and memory retention akin to the role of sleep spindles in NREM2 but at a deeper, more fundamental level.

**Stage 4: REM**

Rapid eye movement (REM) sleep, the final phase in the sleep cycle, is most associated with vivid dreaming. Although REM is often classified alongside NREM3 under the umbrella of slow-wave sleep due to its restorative functions, it is markedly different in terms of brain activity and physiological responses. REM sleep typically ensues about 90 minutes after dozing off, with each cycle extending its length—starting from a brief 10 minutes to potentially an hour in subsequent cycles. Age plays a role in diminishing the duration of REM phases over a lifetime. During REM, the body engages in essential regenerative tasks: fortifying bones, enhancing immune function, and repairing tissues. Concurrently, the brain remains highly active, not only continuing the information processing tasks of NREM3 but also intricately processing emotions. This intensive emotional and psychological processing during REM significantly shapes the themes and emotional tones of dreams, suggesting a critical role in emotional health and psychological balance. The dynamic nature of REM sleep, with its combination of deep physical rest and intense brain activity, underscores its importance in overall well-being, supporting a complex interplay between our physiological and psychological states.

Remarkably, during the REM (Rapid Eye Movement) stage of sleep, the brain exhibits a level of activity that is strikingly similar to its state during wakefulness. This similarity highlights the brain's intense engagement in generating dreams, making REM sleep a phase of profound cognitive activity. Despite the predominance of delta waves, which are characteristic of deep sleep, the occurrence of alpha waves during both NREM3 and the REM phases can result in individuals feeling less revitalized upon waking. This is because alpha waves, often associated with relaxed wakefulness and meditation, may not facilitate the deep restorative processes typically expected from sleep.

In a fascinating contrast to the vibrant activity of the brain, the physical muscles of the body enter a state of complete paralysis during REM sleep. This paralysis serves as a protective mechanism, ensuring that the vivid dreams conjured by the brain do not translate into physical movements, which could potentially lead to injury. This phenomenon of active brain function paired with bodily immobilization has aptly earned REM sleep the nickname "paradoxical sleep." The term encapsulates the curious nature of this sleep stage, where the body is at its most restful state even as the mind continues to explore the boundless realms of dreams.

While the initial sleep stages—NREM1, NREM2, and NREM3—primarily serve the purposes of relaxation and carrying out minor restorative functions, REM sleep stands apart. It is during this phase that the brain consolidates memories, processes emotional experiences, and engages in complex dream narratives. Thus, REM sleep is not only crucial for physical and mental rejuvenation but also presents the optimal condition for lucid dreaming. In lucid dreams, individuals become aware that they are dreaming and can sometimes influence the course of their dreams. This heightened state of consciousness during dreaming is best achieved during REM sleep, due to the unique combination of heightened brain activity and the body's restful paralysis.

## Sleep Paralysis

Sleep paralysis represents a peculiar and sometimes distressing condition where individuals find themselves conscious but unable to move or speak. This state can occur during two key transitions: as one is falling asleep (hypnagogic sleep paralysis) or upon awakening (hypnopompic sleep paralysis). The experience is more frequently reported upon waking. It's noteworthy that approximately 8% of the general population is estimated to encounter sleep paralysis at some point in their lives. However, the prevalence and recurrence of these episodes among individuals, particularly those with sleep disorders such as insomnia, are not fully documented.

Historically, the phenomenon of sleep paralysis was often shrouded in mystery and fear, with many attributing it to supernatural entities or malevolent forces. This interpretation naturally stemmed from the intense vulnerability and vivid hallucinations experienced during such episodes, which could easily be misconstrued as paranormal encounters. Modern science, however, demystifies sleep paralysis by explaining it as a physiological blip in the synchronization between the brain's awakening and the body's ability to move. This insight helps shift the narrative from one of fear to a more rational understanding of sleep paralysis as a natural, albeit uncommon, part of the sleep cycle.

Sleep paralysis is intricately linked to the stages of sleep, particularly REM (rapid eye movement) sleep, during which the body naturally inhibits muscular activity to prevent individuals from acting out their dreams. When this mechanism misfires—leaving the brain alert while the body remains in a state of paralysis—the stage is set for sleep paralysis. The classification into hypnagogic and hypnopompic sleep paralysis helps distinguish whether the episode occurs as one is falling asleep or waking up. Hypnagogic sleep paralysis emerges during the transition into sleep, catching individuals in a limbo of consciousness while the body continues to shut down. On the flip side, hypnopompic sleep paralysis strikes upon waking, when the mind surfaces to consciousness before REM sleep-induced muscle atonia has lifted.

A hallmark of sleep paralysis is the vivid and sometimes terrifying hallucinations that accompany it. These can be auditory, visual, or sensory, blurring the lines between reality and the dream world in a state known as hypnagogia. This term collectively refers to the transitional state between wakefulness and sleep, characterized by vivid, dream-like experiences. Such hallucinations can make an episode of sleep paralysis particularly unsettling, especially when paired with the inability to move or react.

Moreover, sleep paralysis can sometimes intersect with lucid dreaming—the awareness that one is dreaming, with the potential to influence the dream's direction. During sleep paralysis, individuals may report sensations akin to out-of-body experiences or feel detached from their physical selves, accompanied by realistic and sometimes alarming hallucinations. This unique blend of consciousness and immobilization underlines the complexity of sleep paralysis and its adjacent states.

The connection between sleep deprivation and an increased likelihood of experiencing sleep paralysis highlights the importance of maintaining a healthy sleep schedule. Regular, restorative sleep cycles play a crucial role in minimizing the risk of sleep paralysis and enhancing overall well-being.

# CHAPTER 2: WHY DO WE DREAM?

Exploring the enigmatic world of sleep not only enriches our understanding but also ushers us into the complex sphere of lucid dreaming. The fascination with dreams extends back through all of recorded history, weaving its threads into the cultural, artistic, and intellectual tapestry of every civilization known to us. This universal curiosity stems from the remarkable contrast dreams offer to our waking life, providing a nightly escape into countless, vividly imagined worlds. Such enduring intrigue has led to the establishment of oneirology, a specialized field where experts across psychology, neurology, and other scientific domains diligently work to decode this age-old mystery. A landmark in dream research occurred in the mid-20th century when Eugene Aserinsky and Nathaniel Kleitman discovered REM sleep, catalyzing a new era of inquiry into the neurological underpinnings of dreams. This pivotal discovery has since guided the steady advancement of scientific understanding in the realm of sleep studies.

Dreams, irrespective of their nature, are imbued with a variety of inherent benefits. In contrast to the conscious engagement required for lucid dreaming, regular dreams unfold effortlessly, emerging naturally for the vast majority without any deliberate manipulation. This spontaneity suggests a deep-seated purpose behind our nightly visions, as our subconscious minds conjure images, scenarios, and experiences far beyond the confines of our daily existence. The interpretation and significance of these dreams are deeply personal, with individual perceptions varying widely. While some may regard dreams as mere nocturnal distractions, others see them as windows into deeper aspects of the psyche, offering valuable insights and opportunities for personal exploration. The journey into lucid dreaming begins with a mindful examination of these spontaneous dreams, as they can often reveal underlying thoughts, desires, and insights that might otherwise remain obscured.

Beyond the individual exploration of dreams, the collective human fascination with them has led to numerous cultural and philosophical interpretations. Dreams have been viewed as messages from the divine, reflections of inner desires, or even premonitions of future events in various traditions around the world. This rich tapestry of beliefs highlights the multifaceted role dreams play in our lives, serving not only as sources of creative inspiration but also as means for psychological and emotional processing. The process of lucid dreaming, in particular, offers a unique opportunity to interact with and influence these inner narratives directly, providing a powerful tool for self-discovery and personal growth.

As we continue to unravel the mysteries of dreams through both scientific inquiry and personal introspection, we open ourselves to a deeper understanding of the human mind and the limitless potential it holds. Whether through the lens of oneirology, cultural studies, or our own experiences, the exploration of dreams invites us into a world where the boundaries between reality and imagination blur, offering endless possibilities for exploration, understanding, and transformation.

## The Intricacies of Dreams

In the quiet of the night, our brains embark on an extraordinary journey, weaving together intricate narratives filled with imagery, sensations, emotions, and thoughts, all occurring within the depths of our subconscious. This phenomenon is remarkable, especially when we consider our conscious minds' familiarity with the tangible world, contrasted with our subconscious's rich, intangible experiences. Despite our eyes being closed and our bodies at rest in the safety of our beds, we can experience vivid adventures and emotions, demonstrating the brain's exceptional ability to create complex, sensory experiences independently. This capacity for nightly escapades, varying from blissful to nightmarish experiences, underscores the enigmatic nature of dreams and their profound impact on us.

Dreams predominantly unfold during the REM phase of sleep but are not exclusive to it, as they can also manifest during non-REM sleep stages. A notable characteristic of dreaming, particularly during REM sleep, is the heightened activity within the brain's emotional centers, coupled with a reduction in activity within areas responsible for logical reasoning, such as the prefrontal cortex. This imbalance often results in dreams that are vividly surreal and defy logical explanation, diverging significantly from our waking life's rational constraints. Conversely, dreams that occur in non-REM sleep stages tend to possess a more coherent structure and may bear a closer resemblance to real-life events. Common traits observed in REM dreams include:

- Experiencing events from a deeply personal, first-person perspective

- The effortless unfolding of scenarios, arising spontaneously without conscious effort

- The presentation of content that is often surreal, departing significantly from real-life logic

- Engagements with various characters, some familiar and others completely unknown

- The inclusion of elements that reflect the dreamer's personal life and experiences

Investigations into the characters that populate our dreams have revealed that nearly half are individuals we are acquainted with, while others may be recognized solely by their roles or remain entirely anonymous. This discovery highlights the brain's capacity to draw upon a vast repository of stored images and interactions, weaving them into the fabric of our dreams. It's a fascinating testament to the complexity of our subconscious mind and its ability to utilize these reservoirs of memories and impressions in crafting our dream narratives.

Despite some universal themes in the world of dreams, the experience is highly individualized, with variations in color perception, thematic content, and emotional intensity. Some individuals report dreams in vivid color, while others experience them in shades of black and white.

The narrative length and clarity of dreams tend to evolve throughout the night, with initial dreams being shorter and those in later cycles becoming longer and more detailed. On average, a person might journey through three to six dreams each night, with each dream lasting anywhere from five to twenty minutes. Yet, the specialized state of our brain during REM sleep leads to a curious phenomenon where the vivid memories of these nocturnal adventures are often lost upon waking. It's estimated that we forget nearly 95% of our dreams shortly after awakening, leaving us with fleeting fragments of these rich, internal experiences.

This fleeting memory phenomenon raises intriguing questions about the role and significance of dreams in our lives. Are they mere byproducts of the brain's nighttime activity, or do they serve a deeper, perhaps evolutionary, purpose in processing emotions, practicing responses to potential threats, or fostering creativity? As we continue to delve into the mysteries of sleep and dreaming, we inch closer to unraveling the intricate tapestry of the human mind and its capacity for imagination, emotion, and memory.

# The Enigma of Dreams: Exploring Their Purpose and Meaning

The question of why we dream remains one of the most intriguing mysteries in the study of human consciousness. Despite extensive research and theories spanning centuries, a definitive explanation for the occurrence of dreams continues to elude scientists and psychologists alike. Various theories have been proposed, each offering a glimpse into the potential functions and meanings behind our dreams. These theories blend insights from historical psychological perspectives with cutting-edge scientific discoveries, reflecting a broad spectrum of interpretations regarding the purpose of dreams.

Popular theories on the purpose of dreams include:

- **Memory Consolidation:** A widely supported theory suggests that dreams play a crucial role in processing and consolidating memories from our waking lives. This involves reorganizing and integrating new information with existing knowledge, potentially enhancing learning and memory retention.

- **Emotional Processing:** Dreams are believed to provide a virtual stage where emotions can be experienced and processed in diverse scenarios. This emotional rehearsal allows individuals to navigate and resolve feelings and experiences that may be difficult to confront directly in waking life.

- **Cognitive Housekeeping:** Some theories propose that dreaming serves a "clean-up" function for the brain, helping to clear away unnecessary or redundant information accumulated during the day. This neural maintenance ensures that the brain remains efficient and uncluttered.

- **Reflection of Real-Life Scenarios:** Dreams often replay or reinterpret events from our daily lives, allowing the mind to analyze and derive meaning from these experiences. This introspective process may aid in problem-solving and emotional resolution.

- **Existential Byproduct:** There is also a perspective that dreams may simply be a byproduct of the brain's activities during sleep, without serving any specific adaptive purpose. This view posits that dreaming is an incidental outcome of the brain's complex neurochemical processes.

Regardless of the theoretical framework one subscribes to, it is evident that dreams are deeply influenced by the dreamer's personal experiences, relationships, and emotional state. They often contain autobiographical elements, drawing from the individual's memories, desires, and fears.

## Dreams as Therapeutic Instruments

Psychologists have long considered dreams to offer therapeutic benefits, akin to a form of nocturnal therapy. This perspective suggests that dreams allow individuals to confront and process emotions in a safe, abstract environment, often leading to insights and resolutions that might not be accessible in waking life. The reduction of certain stress-related neurochemicals, such as noradrenaline, during REM sleep, provides a calmer backdrop for tackling difficult emotions, potentially facilitating healing and emotional growth.

For example, dreams that evoke fear or anxiety might serve as psychological rehearsals, preparing the individual to face real-life challenges more effectively. This concept is supported by the active role of the amygdala, a brain region associated with processing fear, indicating that dreams might function as simulations for enhancing emotional and survival responses.

## Creativity and Problem-Solving

Another fascinating aspect of dreams is their potential to foster creativity and problem-solving. The less inhibited and emotionally driven nature of thought during REM sleep can lead to innovative ideas and solutions that elude the conscious mind. Historical anecdotes, such as Dmitri Mendeleev's inspiration for the periodic table through a dream, underscore the creative power of dreaming.

## Universal Dream Themes

While dreams are highly individualized, certain themes appear universally across different cultures and populations. These recurring dreams often symbolize common human concerns and psychological states:

- **Falling:** Typically represents feelings of insecurity or anxiety about a particular aspect of one's life.

- **Nudity in Public:** May reflect vulnerability, shame, or a fear of exposure.

- **Being Chased:** Often symbolizes avoidance of a pressing issue or confrontation with fear.

- **Losing Teeth:** Can denote concerns about appearance, communication, or personal power.

- **Flying:** Suggests desires for freedom, control, or escape from constraints.

These themes highlight the complex interplay between our subconscious minds and our waking lives, suggesting that dreams serve as a bridge between our innermost thoughts and our external realities.

## Carl Jung & Sigmund Freud

Carl Jung and Sigmund Freud stand as towering figures in the field of psychology, renowned not just for their foundational contributions but also for their influential theories on the nature and purpose of dreams. While many recognize their roles in shaping psychological thought, the depth of their insights into dreaming and its significance in human development and mental health often goes underappreciated. Despite a once close friendship and professional collaboration, their divergent views on dream interpretation were a source of contention, contributing to the eventual dissolution of their relationship.

Freud's theories on dreams are infamous for their emphasis on the expression of suppressed desires, particularly those of a sexual nature. He posited that dreams serve as an outlet for these repressed urges, allowing them to surface in a state where the usual societal and self-imposed restraints are relaxed. According to Freud, the dream state is a playground where the mind can indulge in its deepest wishes without the constraints of conscious reservation.

Jung, while acknowledging the symbolic nature of dreams as a reflection of the unconscious mind, diverged from Freud's focus on sexual desires. He argued that dreams are not solely preoccupied with our latent sexual cravings but also encompass a broader spectrum of unconscious material. Jung believed that dreams not only allow for the processing and reinterpretation of past experiences but also contain predictive elements, offering foresight into potential future developments of the self. This aspect of his theory suggests that dreams play a crucial role in personal growth and self-realization.

## Types of Dreams

Experts in the field of dream research have delineated five primary categories of dreams, showcasing the diverse experiences our subconscious minds can navigate. These categories underscore the complex interplay between our conscious and subconscious states, revealing the depth and breadth of human cognition and emotion during different stages of rest and daydreaming.

The first category encompasses what we commonly refer to as normal dreams, primarily occurring during the REM phase of sleep. These are the dreams most people are familiar with, characterized by vivid narratives and emotional experiences that can range from joyful to unsettling.

However, a less acknowledged yet equally significant category is that of daydreams. Despite their prevalence, many people might not realize that daydreaming is formally recognized within the spectrum of dreaming. Research suggests that on average, individuals can spend more than 30% of their waking hours immersed in daydreams. This proportion tends to decrease with age, but the phenomenon remains a notable aspect of human cognition. Daydreaming often transpires when our focus shifts away from our immediate surroundings or tasks, propelling us into a contemplative or imaginative state that marginally disconnects us from external stimuli. Within daydreams, there are subcategories: positive-constructive daydreams, filled with hopeful and imaginative content that can foster creativity and potentially ease the path to lucid dreaming; and dysphoric daydreams, which are characterized by anxious or negative thoughts and scenarios, potentially leading to feelings of distress.

The phenomenon of false awakenings forms the third type of dream, where the dreamer is convinced they have awoken and commenced their daily routine, only to later realize the experience was part of a dream. These dreams can be strikingly realistic, blurring the lines between the dream world and reality, and can occur in sequences, further intensifying the confusion between the states of dreaming and waking.

Nightmares make up the fourth category, transforming otherwise normal dreams into deeply frightening experiences. The terror in nightmares is often amplified by the dreamer's lack of awareness that they are in a dream, making the fear and sometimes pain feel exceedingly real. Various factors, such as emotional stress, physical illness, and the consumption of alcohol or certain drugs, can predispose individuals to nightmares. While nightmares are more prevalent in childhood, a small percentage of adults experience chronic nightmares, which may be influenced by medication side effects, dietary habits close to bedtime, or unresolved psychological issues. Increased brain activity due to metabolic processes during sleep might also contribute to the likelihood of experiencing nightmares.

For those suffering from chronic nightmares, the practice of lucid dreaming has been suggested as a therapeutic avenue. Lucid dreaming offers a sense of control and empowerment within the dream, allowing individuals to confront and possibly reshape their nightmarish visions. This technique not only provides a potential relief from the distress caused by nightmares but also opens up new possibilities for exploring and understanding one's subconscious fears and desires.

Beyond these four categories, there's an emerging interest in understanding the role of lucid dreams themselves as a distinct category. Lucid dreaming, where the dreamer becomes aware they are dreaming and can sometimes manipulate the dream's outcome, represents a fascinating intersection of consciousness and subconsciousness. It underscores the brain's remarkable capacity for self-awareness and control even in the depth of sleep, offering invaluable insights into the nature of human consciousness and the potential for cognitive and emotional growth.

## Lucid Dreams

Lucid dreaming occupies a fascinating niche as the fifth and perhaps the most intriguing category of dreams. In this unique state, individuals are not only conscious that they're dreaming but also possess the ability to influence or control the unfolding narrative to varying degrees. This phenomenon represents a pinnacle of dreaming experience, often envied by those who aspire to achieve such awareness and control in their own dreams. Despite the relative rarity of lucid dreams compared to other types, they are accessible to a broad audience, with research indicating that approximately 55% of people have experienced lucid dreaming at some point in their life.

For those unfamiliar with the concept or newcomers to the practice, lucid dreaming can seem daunting, surrounded by misconceptions and fears such as being trapped in a dream, experiencing panic, or even facing life-threatening risks in the waking world. These fears, while understandable, stem from the unknown nature of lucid dreaming to the uninitiated. In reality, lucid dreaming often instills a sense of serenity and empowerment, as the dreamer realizes they have control over the dream environment. This awareness typically dispels fears and provides a comforting reassurance that the experiences within the dream cannot harm them in real life.

Lucid dreaming transcends mere entertainment or wish fulfillment. Many individuals who explore lucid dreaming have a deep connection with their inner psyche and demonstrate a keen awareness of their subconscious, even before delving into lucid dreaming practices. Thus, it is advocated that lucid dreaming be approached with intentions beyond simply living out fantasy scenarios. It offers a unique opportunity to explore personal development, enhance creativity, and gain insights into one's subconscious mind. Lucid dreamers are encouraged to harness this state to broaden their intellectual and emotional horizons, engaging with deeper layers of their psyche that are usually less accessible during waking consciousness.

From a scientific standpoint, lucid dreaming is a goldmine for research into consciousness and brain function. Notably, the prefrontal cortex, a region associated with complex cognitive behavior, personality expression, decision-making, and moderating social behavior, shows increased activity during lucid dreams. This heightened activation suggests that our brains are capable of engaging in logical thought processes and self-reflection during lucid dreams, a stark contrast to the often illogical and whimsical nature of regular dreaming. This bridging of conscious and subconscious realms offers invaluable insights into the capabilities and plasticity of the human mind.

Mastering the art of lucid dreaming, particularly the aspect of control, is both the most challenging and rewarding part of the practice. Even experienced lucid dreamers sometimes find it difficult to maintain complete dominance over their dream states, with certain elements remaining under subconscious influence. Initially, a dreamer might find they can dictate their actions or alter specific aspects of the dream while other parts continue independently of their will. However, as one becomes more adept and comfortable within the lucid dreaming space, their ability to navigate and influence the dream world tends to improve. With practice, the boundaries of dream control expand, allowing for more profound exploration and interaction with the dreamer's subconscious desires, fears, and aspirations.

Lucid dreaming not only challenges our understanding of the dreaming mind but also offers a powerful tool for personal exploration and growth. It stands as a testament to the untapped potential of the human mind, inviting us to explore the depths of our consciousness in a space where the limitations of physical reality do not bind us. For those willing to embark on this journey, lucid dreaming can open the door to unparalleled self-discovery and transformation.

## History of Lucid Dreaming

The concept of lucid dreaming was formally introduced in 1913 by the Dutch psychiatrist Frederik van Eeden, although significant scientific exploration into the phenomenon gained momentum much later, primarily from the 1960s through the 1980s. Yet, the origins and applications of lucid dreaming extend beyond the confines of scientific inquiry. While lucid dreaming is intrinsically connected to the biological mechanisms of the human brain, individuals across various cultures and spiritual traditions have harnessed it for purposes ranging from spiritual enlightenment to pure entertainment.

The intersection of spirituality and lucid dreaming is notably profound. In Buddhist traditions, for instance, practitioners engage in lucid dreaming as a method to deepen their spiritual connections. This involves cultivating awareness within the dream state to perform tasks that contribute to personal and spiritual growth. Practitioners might use lucid dreaming to confront personal fears, or they may seek interactions with spiritual entities as part of their inner journey. The use of lucid dreaming for spiritual exploration and personal development is a practice with ancient roots, spanning across diverse cultures and spiritual traditions for millennia.

Many individuals who integrate lucid dreaming into their spiritual practice also incorporate meditation into their daily lives, creating a synergistic effect between their waking and dreaming states. This combination of meditation and lucid dreaming enhances the ability to navigate the dream world with intentionality, opening up avenues for profound self-discovery and spiritual growth. Through this holistic approach, lucid dreaming becomes not just an intriguing phenomenon of the sleeping brain but a powerful tool for personal and spiritual exploration, bridging the gap between the conscious and subconscious realms.

# CHAPTER 3: HOW TO LUCID DREAM

A diverse array of individuals, extending beyond the confines of academic expertise in neuroscience, psychology, or the study of dreams, express a keen interest in lucid dreaming for myriad personal reasons. This interest spans spiritual exploration, cognitive enhancement, healing from trauma, and the pursuit of expanded life experiences. From the vantage point of researchers, engaging more deeply with lucid dreaming not only enriches personal development but also promises to shed light on the intricate relationship between our conscious and subconscious minds. Notably, lucid dreaming has found its place as an innovative therapeutic approach, especially for individuals coping with post-traumatic stress disorder (PTSD). The ability to consciously navigate and modify the narrative of nightmares provides a valuable mechanism for alleviating the intensity and frequency of these distressing episodes.

Despite the benefits, there are reservations about lucid dreaming, particularly concerning the potential for individuals to blur the distinction between dream-induced realities and the waking world. This underscores the importance of approaching lucid dreaming not as an escape from reality, but as a means to enhance personal insight and mental resilience. For those venturing into lucid dreaming independently, without the guidance of a therapist or professional, laying a solid mental and emotional groundwork is essential. This foundation is built on introspection, a readiness to confront and engage with one's subconscious, and an absence of fear or skepticism. A disconnect from one's deeper subconscious may lead to challenging or even negative lucid dreaming experiences, emphasizing the necessity of a healthy, open mindset as a precursor to successful lucid dreaming. Studies support the notion that an individual's receptiveness to and desire for lucid dreaming significantly influences its occurrence, highlighting the powerful connection between psychological readiness and the capacity for lucid experiences.

Spiritually inclined individuals often find themselves at an advantage in achieving lucid dreams, thanks to their ongoing engagement with the deeper aspects of their minds. For example, Buddhist monks, who practice lucid dreaming as an extension of their spiritual exercises, frequently incorporate meditation into their daily routines. This practice generates alpha brain waves not only during the initial stages of non-REM sleep but also throughout the day, effectively priming the brain for lucid dreaming. This integration of meditation and lucid dreaming enriches the practitioners' spiritual journey, enhancing their understanding of the self and the universe. The blending of these practices underlines the monks' ability to seamlessly navigate between wakefulness, meditation, and dreaming, thereby cultivating a more profound connection to their spiritual essence.

In addition to spiritual practices, lucid dreaming can also serve as a unique avenue for creative exploration and problem-solving. Many artists, writers, and inventors have reported finding inspiration for their work within the lucid dream state, tapping into the unrestricted creativity of the subconscious mind. Lucid dreaming offers a limitless canvas for experimentation and discovery, allowing individuals to explore scenarios, concepts, and solutions that may seem unreachable in the constraints of waking reality.

## Embarking on the Journey

For individuals who find themselves unable to remember or feel connected to their dreams, the journey toward lucid dreaming is just beginning. If you're starting from scratch, it's crucial to first become acquainted with the dreams you're already having before attempting to achieve lucidity. Without the ability to recall your nightly dreams, attempting lucid dreaming techniques might prove futile, as it indicates a disconnect from your dream world. To bridge this gap, the initial step involves familiarizing yourself with the natural dreamscape crafted by your subconscious, setting the stage for you to eventually take control.

## Enhancing Dream Recall

It's a common experience: you awaken from a dream, convinced of its significance and certain you'll remember it, only to find it fading away as you start your day. This frustrating phenomenon, where vivid dream memories vanish almost instantly, can leave you feeling unsettled. While the fleeting nature of dream recall is partly due to our brain's chemistry, there are strategies to improve memory retention of dreams, an essential skill for those aspiring to lucid dreaming.

Dreams, especially during the REM phase, tend to increase in duration as the night progresses, making later stages prime for vivid dreaming. Understanding this pattern can help you anticipate when you're most likely to experience REM sleep. Awakening directly from REM sleep significantly boosts the chances of remembering your dreams in detail. Strategically setting an alarm for the last two hours of sleep can enhance your dream recall. Initially, interrupting a dream might seem counterproductive, but reentering a dream after briefly waking is more manageable during REM sleep.

Setting a clear intention before sleep can also fortify dream recall. Simply reminding yourself, "I will remember my dream tonight," as you drift off can prime your brain to hold onto those dream details more firmly. This practice may require persistence, but many have found success with this straightforward method.

Your physical position upon waking can also influence recall. Remaining in the same posture as when you first awaken can help cement dream memories. If you need to move, such as to silence an alarm, try to return to your original position to aid memory retrieval. Sometimes, dreams leave behind a fragment—a face, a place, or a piece of clothing. By focusing on these details and asking yourself questions about them, you can sometimes unravel a larger narrative. Even a lingering emotion from a dream can act as a key to unlocking more comprehensive memories.

Maintaining a dream journal is perhaps the most effective technique for enhancing dream recall. Write down everything you can remember upon waking, focusing not only on the visual aspects but also on the emotions and themes. This practice, done with consistency, not only trains your brain to remember more details over time but also familiarizes you with the landscape of your dreams, revealing patterns and recurring symbols.

Through these methods, you can develop a closer relationship with your dreams, transforming fleeting night visions into vivid memories that enrich your understanding of your subconscious mind and pave the way for lucid dreaming experiences.

## Reality Testing: A Gateway to Lucid Dreaming

Mastering the ability to discern between the dream world and waking reality is an essential skill for those interested in lucid dreaming. On the surface, distinguishing between dreams and reality might seem straightforward, but dreams often mimic real-life experiences with such fidelity that identifying them as dreams becomes a challenge. This is where reality testing, a deliberate technique to determine if you are in a dream, becomes invaluable.

Our dreams, despite their vividness and complexity, sometimes lack the granularity and consistency of the real world. This discrepancy lies in the brain's occasional failure to replicate fine details accurately within the dream state. By becoming adept at identifying these inconsistencies through reality testing, you can more easily recognize when you are dreaming. Some practical reality testing strategies include:

- **Hand Examination:** Take a moment to closely inspect your hands, look away briefly, then inspect them again. A dream state might reveal anomalies, such as fluctuating numbers of fingers or a blurred appearance, because the dreaming brain struggles with maintaining consistent visual details.

- **Defying Physics:** Attempt actions that defy the laws of physics, like trying to pass your hand through a solid object. Success in such tasks clearly indicates a dream state, as such phenomena are impossible in the physical world.

- **Text Reading Challenge:** Engaging with text in dreams—either by reading or speaking it aloud—is often fraught with difficulty. The dream state impairs the brain's ability to process written language coherently, making this an effective test for lucidity.

- **Technology Interaction:** Operating digital devices in dreams usually results in unusual malfunctions or surreal behaviors, reflecting the dream brain's incomplete understanding of how these devices function in reality.

- **Clock Observation:** Clocks and timepieces in dreams are notoriously unreliable. Their inability to display time consistently, along with odd appearances or behaviors, signals the dreaming brain's struggle with linear time concepts.

- **Light Switch Test:** Trying to manipulate lighting conditions, such as turning lights on or off, often reveals dream states through switches that behave unpredictably or have no effect.

Reality testing hinges on our understanding of how the brain constructs the dream environment, often failing to replicate specific, familiar aspects of waking life accurately. Regularly performing reality checks during the day increases the chances of conducting them in your dreams, thereby promoting lucidity.

The nuanced creativity of the subconscious mind in dreams sometimes omits precise details, partly because the left hemisphere—responsible for logical thinking and detail-oriented analysis—remains less active during sleep. Identifying dream signs that demand attention to detail can thus become easier. Intriguingly, upon achieving lucidity within a dream, the left hemisphere can re-engage, enhancing logical thinking and the accuracy of dream details, which may eventually diminish the efficacy of reality checks as the dream progresses.

Incorporating reality testing into your daily routine not only primes you for recognizing when you are dreaming but also deepens your engagement with the inner workings of your subconscious. This practice doesn't just pave the way for more controlled and meaningful lucid dreaming experiences; it fosters a richer understanding of the mind's vast capabilities and the seamless continuum between our conscious and subconscious lives. Through diligent application of these techniques, lucid dreaming can transform from an elusive phenomenon into a navigable and profoundly insightful aspect of your mental landscape.

## Identifying Dream Signs

Dream signs are unique or improbable events within a dream that signal you're not in the waking world. Inspired by cultural references like the film "Inception," where the protagonist uses a spinning top to test reality—spinning indefinitely in a dream versus stopping in reality—dream signs can range from the blatantly obvious to the subtly nuanced. For instance, the ability to fly or finding oneself at a much younger age than in reality are indicators that one is dreaming.

Dream signs fall into three primary categories:

- **Anomalies:** These are unusual or singular events that stand out because they defy normal logic or experience, such as an elephant barking.

- **Dream Themes:** Common motifs or scenarios that frequently occur across many people's dreams, like the experience of being naked in public.

- **Recurring Signs:** Personal and specific to the individual, these signs appear repeatedly across different dreams and may serve as a personal cue to the dreamer that they are in a dream state.

Recognizing your own unique dream signs is a crucial step towards differentiating between the dream world and reality. Achieving awareness of these signs while dreaming can significantly increase the likelihood of triggering lucidity. Maintaining a dream journal facilitates the recognition of personal themes and recurring signs, making it easier to identify when you're dreaming. By becoming intimately familiar with your dream signs, you can actively look for them in your dreams, enhancing your ability to become lucid and navigate the dream world with greater awareness.

## Exploring Lucid Dreaming Techniques

Over the years, experts in various fields, whether for scholarly research or therapeutic purposes, have developed numerous techniques to induce lucid dreaming. This array of strategies offers individuals the opportunity to experiment and find the method that resonates best with them. Given that these techniques are still under preliminary investigation, their effectiveness is highly individualized.

## Mnemonic Induction of Lucid Dreams (MILD)

Stephen LaBerge, a renowned psychophysiologist with a deep focus on lucid dreaming, is a pivotal figure in this area of study. His development of the Mnemonic Induction of Lucid Dreams (MILD) technique has significantly impacted the practice of lucid dreaming. MILD leverages memory, particularly prospective memory—the intention to remember to perform actions in the future—to achieve lucidity within dreams. This technique, which incorporates elements of visualization, self-hypnosis, and memory, is considered one of the most effective paths to lucid dreaming.

LaBerge's inspiration for MILD draws on historical lucid dreaming practices dating back to the 16th century, showcasing the long-standing human fascination with understanding and navigating the dream world. MILD specifically emphasizes dream recall and the strategic use of prospective memory. Practitioners are encouraged to vividly recall a dream they've had, pinpointing a scene containing a dream sign, such as an unusual or impossible object or scenario. For instance, recalling the vision of a deformed clock and intensely focusing on this image before falling asleep sets the stage for lucidity. The next step involves setting a firm intention to recognize you're dreaming when encountering such anomalies in your dream, thereby increasing the likelihood of achieving lucidity during subsequent REM sleep phases.

Prospective memory, fundamental to the MILD technique, is a common aspect of our daily lives. It's what enables us to remember future tasks without conscious effort, such as waking up at a specific time without an alarm. This form of memory keeps our brain alert to our intentions on a subconscious level, enhancing the chance of realizing when we are dreaming. By harnessing the power of prospective memory in conjunction with deliberate intention setting and visualization, individuals can significantly boost their ability to become lucid within their dreams.

The MILD technique's emphasis on intentionality and memory underscores the intricate relationship between our waking and dreaming consciousness. By actively engaging with our dreams through techniques like MILD, we open up new avenues for self-exploration, creativity, and insight into our subconscious mind.

## Wake-Initiated Lucid Dream (WILD)

The Wake-Initiated Lucid Dream (WILD) technique is among the more challenging yet insightful pathways into lucid dreaming, offering an intimate exploration of the transition from consciousness into the dream state. This process begins by interrupting one's sleep after four to six hours, ensuring a brief period of wakefulness before attempting to re-enter sleep with a conscious intent to remain aware. As you recline, envision your body gradually dissolving or sinking into the bed, a visualization that fosters deep relaxation and primes you for entry into the dream world. During this delicate juncture, you may encounter hypnagogic hallucinations, which are visual or auditory sensations that occur as you're about to enter the dream state while maintaining awareness. These can range from simple patterns to complex scenes and serve as precursors to full lucidity.

As you delve deeper, sleep paralysis might set in—a natural, albeit often unsettling, phenomenon where the body becomes immobile as a part of the sleep cycle. It's crucial to approach this phase with calm and see it as a progression towards achieving a WILD. Following sleep paralysis, many practitioners report experiencing sensations akin to leaving their physical body or the spontaneous generation of a dream environment, often mirroring their actual surroundings. Given the potential for intense experiences like sleep paralysis, the WILD technique is best suited for those with a solid foundation in lucid dreaming and a composed mindset.

### Senses Initiated Lucid Dream (SSILD)

The Senses Initiated Lucid Dream (SSILD) technique is a practice that capitalizes on sensory engagement to trigger lucidity. Like MILD, it involves waking after approximately five hours of sleep but focuses on immersing oneself in the present sensory environment rather than recalling previous dreams. During the brief moments of wakefulness, you're encouraged to pay acute attention to your senses—observing the play of light behind closed eyelids, the ambient sounds, or the feel of your bedding against your skin. This deep sensory immersion before returning to sleep sets the stage for a lucid dreaming experience, as the brain continues to process these stimuli within the dream.

SSILD promotes a lucid dreaming approach grounded in environmental awareness, making it a tangible and accessible method for many. By directing attention to external stimuli, the technique nurtures a seamless integration of waking consciousness into the dream state, enhancing the likelihood of lucidity.

### Dream Initiated Lucid Dream (DILD)

Differing from techniques that start with wakefulness, the Dream Initiated Lucid Dream (DILD) method begins from within the dream itself. It leverages the dreamer's capacity for in-dream recognition of anomalies or out-of-place elements as a springboard into lucidity. This approach might involve identifying oddities in dream objects or scenarios—anything from the impossible physics of floating objects to the presence of incongruent symbols.

The core of DILD lies in the practice of reality checks—routine questioning of one's environment both in waking life and within the dream—to cultivate an awareness that can spark lucidity. For instance, noticing inconsistencies in the behavior of hands, the passage of time, or the legibility of text can indicate that you're dreaming, facilitating a shift into lucid awareness. This technique encourages dreamers to actively engage with their dream environment, applying critical observation skills to trigger the realization of dreaming.

# CHAPTER 4: LUCID DREAMING BENEFITS

Lucid dreaming transcends the realm of mere nocturnal escapades, offering profound benefits that positively influence various aspects of waking life. This fascinating state of consciousness, where one becomes aware and can exert control within dreams, not only enriches the quality of sleep but also carries over substantial mental, emotional, and even physical health benefits into daily existence.

The empowerment experienced through the deliberate manipulation of dream environments in lucid dreaming often parallels an increased sense of control and confidence in waking life. Individuals who regularly engage in lucid dreaming report a noticeable decrease in anxiety and stress. This is attributed to the practice of navigating and overcoming obstacles within the dream world, which translates to a more composed and proactive approach to real-life challenges. The habitual experience of controlling outcomes and facing fears in dreams teaches lucid dreamers to perceive situations in their waking lives as within their influence, reducing feelings of helplessness and anxiety.

Beyond the psychological benefits, lucid dreaming has been observed to stimulate unique patterns of brain activity, fostering novel neural connections and enhancing the interplay between different brain regions. During lucid dreaming, areas of the brain responsible for self-awareness, decision-making, and emotional regulation become more active than during regular dreaming or waking states. This alteration in brain function can lead to improved cognitive abilities, including enhanced creativity, problem-solving skills, and memory retention. The practice of lucid dreaming serves as a form of mental training, reinforcing neural pathways that contribute to a sharper, more agile mind.

Additionally, lucid dreaming offers a unique platform for personal growth and self-exploration. It provides a safe space to confront personal fears, rehearse challenging scenarios, and work through unresolved issues. This can lead to greater emotional stability and insight into one's behavior and thought patterns, fostering a deeper understanding of oneself and facilitating personal development.

Physical health can also indirectly benefit from the practice of lucid dreaming. The relaxation and stress reduction achieved through lucid dreaming can improve sleep quality, leading to better overall physical health. Moreover, the visualization techniques practiced in lucid dreaming have been suggested to potentially aid in physical rehabilitation and pain management, as the mind-body connection is harnessed to promote healing.

## Unlocking Creativity Through Lucid Dreaming

Lucid dreaming goes beyond the exhilaration of navigating dreams at will; it offers a profound avenue for enhancing creativity, insight, and problem-solving abilities in waking life. While the direct correlation between lucid dreaming and an increase in measurable intelligence may still be under investigation, substantial evidence underscores its significant impact on boosting creativity and fostering an insightful mindset. Engaging in lucid dreaming propels the dreamer into a world unbound by the physical laws and societal norms that govern waking reality, not only enabling extraordinary experiences but also directly enriching cognitive function. This is due in part to the enhanced neural connectivity fostered by lucid dreaming, particularly between the brain's frontopolar cortex and temporoparietal junction, areas pivotal to creative thought and problem-solving. Studies suggest individuals who practice lucid dreaming exhibit a remarkable ability to solve up to 25% more problems, highlighting the technique's potential for cognitive enhancement.

Beyond the realms of deep sleep, the transitional states of hypnagogia (the threshold between wakefulness and sleep) and hypnopompia (the transition from sleep to waking) serve as fertile grounds for creative exploration. The hypnagogic state, in particular, is a crucible of creativity, where the day's memories meld with fantasies, daydreams, and subconscious musings to produce novel and sometimes whimsical ideas. This blending of cognitive elements can spark innovative problem-solving strategies and creative insights, making the hypnagogic state a valuable resource for those seeking to push the boundaries of their imagination.

Historical anecdotes abound with luminaries such as Dmitri Mendeleev and Thomas Edison leveraging these states for breakthrough discoveries and inventions. Edison's innovative technique of inducing the hypnagogic state to capture fleeting moments of inspiration underscores the practical applications of understanding and utilizing these unique states of consciousness. By embracing the creative chaos of the hypnagogic state, Edison was able to conceptualize the design breakthrough that led to the development of the light bulb.

The hypnopompic state, experienced as the mind emerges from the depths of sleep, offers a similarly potent opportunity for insight and innovation. This period of waking, characterized by a refreshed and unburdened mind following a night of dreaming and subconscious processing, can yield profound clarity and spontaneous ideas. To harness the full potential of this state, it is advisable to remain still and mentally open upon awakening, allowing any emerging thoughts or insights to surface naturally. This gentle approach can reveal unexpected solutions and creative ideas that may not have been accessible during the analytical rigor of daytime thought processes.

To further enrich the creative benefits of these transitional sleep states, individuals are encouraged to cultivate practices that enhance dream recall and awareness, such as maintaining a dream journal and performing regular reality checks. By becoming more attuned to the nuances of their dream experiences and the unique cognitive landscape of sleep, dreamers can unlock new levels of creativity, insight, and problem-solving prowess.

In essence, lucid dreaming and the exploration of hypnagogic and hypnopompic states represent a holistic approach to cognitive and creative enhancement. By bridging the gap between the conscious and subconscious mind, individuals can access a wellspring of innovative ideas, solve complex problems with newfound ease, and enrich their waking life with the boundless creativity born from the depths of their dreams.

## Enhancing Physical Abilities Through Lucid Dreaming

The concept of mental rehearsal or visualization to enhance physical performance is well-established in the realm of athletics. Athletes from various disciplines have successfully used mental practice to refine their skills, rehearse routines, and improve their performance during actual competitions. This technique underscores the profound connection between the mind's visualization capabilities and physical execution, suggesting that the act of mentally rehearsing movements can significantly impact an athlete's ability to perform them in reality. Lucid dreaming, with its unique ability to simulate realistic experiences while asleep, extends this principle into new territories, offering potential benefits for physical rehabilitation and skill enhancement.

Pioneering research into the potential of lucid dreaming for physical well-being, conducted by luminaries such as Ed Kellogg and Robert Waggoner, explores how the deep immersion in vivid, controlled dream environments can influence physical healing and skill development. Their findings highlight the placebo effect's power—where the belief in a treatment's efficacy, absent any active ingredient, can lead to tangible health improvements. In the context of lucid dreaming, this translates to the mind's ability to conceive and engage in detailed physical activities, potentially accelerating healing and enhancing motor skills through the psychosomatic connection, the intricate link between psychological processes and physical states.

This psychosomatic connection posits that the mind and body are not separate entities, but part of a cohesive system where psychological states can directly influence physical health and vice versa. Lucid dreaming serves as a powerful tool to strengthen this connection, enabling individuals to consciously explore and influence their physical state through mental processes. For instance, the phenomenon where fear-induced perception, devoid of any real threat, can increase heart rate exemplifies how mental states can manifest as physical responses in the body. Lucid dreaming amplifies this concept, allowing for the deliberate mental rehearsal of physical activities that could induce positive physiological changes and improvements in motor skills.

Moreover, the practice of lucid dreaming for physical enhancement does not stop at mere visualization. It offers a sandbox for experimenting with movements and actions that may be currently limited or impossible due to injury, disability, or skill level, providing a safe space for exploration and adaptation. The repeated mental practice of these movements in the lucid dream state can lead to neural adaptations and improvements in motor execution in waking life, much like physical practice would.

Lucid dreaming also presents an opportunity for overcoming mental barriers to physical performance, such as fear, anxiety, or a lack of confidence. By facing and conquering these challenges within the dream, individuals can translate that confidence and resilience to their waking lives, potentially breaking through plateaus in physical performance or recovery.

In summary, the intersection of mental visualization, lucid dreaming, and physical performance encapsulates a holistic approach to enhancing physical abilities. By harnessing the mind's power to simulate and rehearse physical activities within the dream state, individuals can potentially catalyze improvements in motor skills, accelerate healing processes, and overcome psychological barriers to physical performance. This synergy between mind and body, mediated through lucid dreaming, opens up new avenues for physical therapy, sports training, and overall wellness, underscoring the untapped potential of our subconscious minds in influencing our physical realities.

## Addressing and Alleviating Nightmares through Lucid Dreaming and Imagery Rehearsal Therapy

While chronic nightmares are relatively uncommon, it's estimated that up to 85% of people will experience them occasionally. These intense, disturbing dreams can evoke strong emotional responses, leading individuals to awaken feeling distressed, unrested, and potentially carrying the emotional burden into their waking lives. The impact of nightmares extends beyond the immediate aftermath, potentially affecting an individual's mental well-being for days at a time. Furthermore, the fear of recurring nightmares can lead to sleep avoidance, creating a vicious cycle where the dread of falling asleep exacerbates the problem, reducing sleep quality and contributing to heightened levels of stress and anxiety.

Lucid dreaming offers a transformative approach to managing and overcoming the fear associated with recurring nightmares. By cultivating the ability to become conscious within the dream state, individuals can recognize the illusory nature of the nightmare, stripping it of its power to terrify. Gaining control within the dream not only neutralizes its negative emotional impact but also empowers the dreamer, providing a profound sense of agency. This empowerment can extend into waking life, bolstering confidence and resilience in the face of challenges.

Imagery Rehearsal Therapy (IRT) is a psychological technique employed by therapists to aid individuals in reshaping the narrative of their nightmares. This therapeutic approach involves the patient actively reimagining their recurring nightmare with a more positive, empowering outcome. By mentally rehearsing this revised narrative during therapy sessions, the individual's mind is trained to recognize the dream as just that—a dream. This recognition empowers them to apply the technique in their sleep, allowing for conscious control over the dream's direction and outcome.

IRT not only helps in altering the content of nightmares but also in reducing their frequency. By practicing a new, positive storyline, individuals can gradually diminish the emotional impact of their nightmares, leading to improved sleep quality and overall mental health. Additionally, this method reinforces the individual's belief in their ability to influence their dream content, further reducing the fear of sleep and the potential for nightmares.

Beyond IRT, engaging in relaxation techniques before bed, maintaining a regular sleep schedule, and creating a sleep-conducive environment can also play crucial roles in preventing nightmares. These practices, combined with lucid dreaming techniques, offer a comprehensive strategy for individuals seeking relief from the distress caused by nightmares.

# CHAPTER 5: EXPLORING THE DREAM WORLD

With the wealth of lucid dreaming techniques readily accessible, the realm of lucid dreaming unfurls before you, offering an expansive universe of possibilities. By applying these methods with precision and cultivating patience, you can unlock a personal domain of lucid dreams. Armed with determination and the correct mindset, the bounds of reality dissolve, enabling the actualization of your most extravagant dreams and desires.

Dreams are inherently vivid tapestries woven from the threads of our emotions, and lucid dreams are no exception. Within the lucid dream state, we find ourselves emboldened to undertake activities and adventures far beyond our waking considerations. Some theorists propose that our dreams serve as mirrors to our unconscious, revealing our deepest, often unacknowledged desires and motivations. It's within these nocturnal narratives that our suppressed yearnings and instinctual drives—be they related to sexuality, aggression, or other primal urges—come to the forefront. This phenomenon, known as the dream rebound effect, illustrates how our subconscious mind navigates and expresses repressed desires more freely during sleep. Engaging with these aspects of our psyche within the controlled environment of a lucid dream offers a constructive and healthy outlet for exploring and understanding these deep-seated inclinations.

The sanctuary of lucid dreams provides a unique space where judgement is suspended, and exploration is encouraged. Here, the near-limitless control available to the dreamer allows for a profound personal journey into the subconscious. Initially, newcomers to lucid dreaming might find their awareness heightened within the dream, yet may encounter challenges in steering the dream's direction. Over time, with practice and perseverance, the ability to manipulate and shape the dream landscape grows, enabling dreamers to orchestrate their experiences with increasing finesse.

As mastery over lucid dreaming progresses, individuals gain not just the ability to fulfill their fantasies or confront their fears but also the opportunity to engage in creative problem-solving, rehearse for real-life situations, or simply bask in the exhilaration of unrestrained freedom. The therapeutic potential of lucid dreaming is vast, offering avenues for psychological healing, overcoming personal barriers, and fostering growth and self-awareness.

Furthermore, the immersive experience of lucid dreaming can contribute to skill development and learning. By practicing physical or mental tasks within a dream, individuals can effect real-world improvements in their abilities, illustrating the powerful connection between the mind's dream activities and its waking functions.

To fully harness the potential of lucid dreaming, it's crucial to cultivate a disciplined approach to dream journaling, reality checks, and mindfulness practices. These foundational techniques not only enhance dream recall and awareness but also facilitate deeper engagement with the dream world, allowing dreamers to navigate their subconscious landscapes with clarity and purpose.

In essence, the journey into lucid dreaming is a journey into the self, offering a reflective mirror to our innermost thoughts, desires, and potentials. Through dedicated practice and a willingness to explore the depths of our minds, we can unlock the transformative power of lucid dreaming, discovering within it a rich source of insight, creativity, and personal growth.

## Mastering Control in Lucid Dreams

One of the most challenging aspects of lucid dreaming is achieving the realization that you're within a dream. Once this awareness is established, the pathway to manipulating your dream environment becomes increasingly accessible. Initially, you may find yourself in what's known as an uncontrolled lucid dream, where your awareness of the dream state doesn't extend to control over the dream's content. In such dreams, your influence is limited to your actions, much like in your waking life. This stage is a normal part of the learning curve for beginners and doesn't reflect a shortfall in technique; rather, it's an essential step towards gaining fuller control over your dreams. Mastery over your dream world typically develops with continued practice and enhanced mindfulness.

Enhancing control over your lucid dreams involves a crucial principle: striking a balance between your conscious will and the spontaneous creations of your subconscious. This process requires keen observation and discernment, assessing the elements of your dream to align them with your intended outcomes. By actively engaging with the details of your dream and expressing a clear intention to modify them, you signal to your brain that these elements hold significance, and that your conscious self is prepared to steer the dream narrative. Verbalizing your desires within the dream, confidently stating the changes you wish to manifest, can also catalyze these alterations. With persistence and belief in the efficacy of these actions, you'll begin to notice shifts in your dream environment that reflect your intentions.

Over time, as you refine these techniques, the necessity to consciously direct every aspect of the dream diminishes. Your subconscious mind gradually becomes more receptive to your guidance, allowing for a more seamless integration of conscious control within the dream landscape. The sections that follow delve into various facets of your dream that you may learn to manipulate and offer strategies for exercising control over them.

## Interacting with Characters in Lucid Dreams

Individuals populate our dreams regularly, whether in lucid states or ordinary ones. They can range from loved ones and close acquaintances to vague, unfamiliar figures who play peripheral roles in our dream narratives. Regardless of their significance, these characters can either facilitate or hinder the progression of the storyline you envision for your lucid dream. Hence, mastering how to influence dream characters and their behaviors can enhance your lucid dreaming experience.

To modify the actions or presence of people in your lucid dreams, start by engaging in a detailed observation. Consider questions like: Who are these individuals? What is their stance or position within the dream? Can you describe their attire in detail? What expressions do they wear on their faces? Such inquiries heighten your consciousness within the dream and subtly influence your subconscious to grant you the ability to manipulate these aspects.

The realm of lucid dreaming is boundless, extending this limitless potential to the control over dream characters as well. Seasoned lucid dreamers have the capability to alter dream characters—transforming their identities, dictating their responses, or aligning them with the dreamer's goals within the dream scenario. Even the physical appearances and personalities of these characters are malleable. However, with great power comes great responsibility; it is crucial to exercise this control with mindfulness and respect for the narrative integrity.

Lucid dreaming is heralded for its therapeutic advantages, particularly as a method for individuals to explore, understand, and reinterpret their relationships from an innovative perspective. Consequently, many aim to consciously incorporate specific individuals from their waking life into their dreamscapes. Preparing for this involves concentrating on the intended person prior to sleep and upon achieving lucidity. The accuracy with which these figures appear in dreams often correlates with the dreamer's familiarity with them, enabling a highly realistic representation. To fulfill the therapeutic intent of reassessing real-world interactions, it's advisable to preserve the genuine personality and traits of the individuals depicted in your dreams.

This nuanced approach to character interaction in lucid dreams not only enriches the dreaming experience but also offers a unique avenue for personal insight and emotional resolution. By thoughtfully engaging with the characters that populate your dreams, you unlock the potential for profound understanding and growth, reflecting the complex interplay between our subconscious minds and our waking relationships.

## Mastering Environment Control in Lucid Dreams

Manipulating the setting is a coveted aspect of lucid dreaming, offering dreamers the chance to immerse themselves in environments far beyond the constraints of the physical world. Whether it's exploring distant lands or venturing into realms that defy earthly existence, achieving this level of control in lucid dreams is a sought-after experience. A fundamental step towards enhancing your ability to shape dreamscapes involves a deep awareness and appreciation of the details in your current dream environment, even those beyond your control.

Upon realizing you're in a dream, immerse yourself in the sensory and aesthetic nuances around you. Question the hue of the sky, the texture of the ground beneath your feet, or the reason a particular scenery evokes certain emotions. Such meticulous observation not only enriches your dreaming experience but also primes your subconscious for transformation.

Should you wish to alter your surroundings, focusing intently on every detail you wish to change is key. Visualize vividly how you want the new setting to appear, channeling your energy into this mental image. Changes might manifest incrementally, allowing you to witness the creative process of each element reassembling according to your vision, or they may materialize instantaneously, transforming your dream world in the blink of an eye.

One straightforward strategy for environment alteration in lucid dreams is to envision yourself traveling to a new location. For instance, if you desire to swap a familiar setting for a majestic castle, picture it nearby, compelling you to embark on a journey within your dream to reach this fantastical destination. For those seeking more radical environmental shifts, employing methods like teleportation or flight offers a thrilling and efficient means of dream travel. The sensation of flying, particularly, is celebrated in lucid dreams for its exhilarating freedom and defiance of real-world limitations.

For more experienced lucid dreamers, creating portals represents an advanced technique for scene transition. Similar to teleportation, this method involves conjuring a portal that serves as a gateway to your desired dreamscape.

Mastering the art of environment control in lucid dreams unlocks endless possibilities for exploration and adventure. By training your mind to notice, appreciate, and then alter the details of your dream world, you open the door to limitless creativity and personal fulfillment. This practice not only enhances the vividness and variety of your dream experiences but also empowers you to explore the depths of your imagination, discovering new facets of your subconscious mind.

## Storyline

To explore new dimensions of their experiences or challenge their capabilities, individuals who engage in lucid dreaming often aspire to master control over the dream's narrative. The narrative framework of a lucid dream is intricately woven from elements involving both characters and settings. By acquiring proficiency in manipulating these components, you inherently gain the ability to steer the overarching storyline of your dream. The subsequent step involves mastering control over the progression of events that are independent of your direct involvement.

For instance, if you're intrigued by the idea of immersing yourself in a storyline reminiscent of cinematic adventures, you'll need to learn how to orchestrate events beyond your immediate actions. To start harnessing this level of narrative control, begin with manageable objectives. For example, envision yourself soaring through the sky while guiding a flock of birds to accompany you. As you refine your skills and expand your imaginative influence, you'll gradually be able to facilitate events of increasing complexity and drama, tailored to your creative desires.

This evolution in control from simple acts to complex narrative orchestration underscores the limitless potential of lucid dreaming. With practice and determination, you can transition from influencing personal actions and interactions to curating elaborate, movie-like scenarios, enriching your lucid dreaming experience with depth and diversity. This journey not only enhances your ability to navigate the dream world with greater finesse but also deepens your understanding of the boundless creativity and storytelling power housed within your subconscious mind.

## Guidelines for a Positive Lucid Dreaming Experience

Navigating the realm of lucid dreaming with awareness and caution is crucial for ensuring a fulfilling and positive experience. While lucid dreaming offers a spectrum of incredible benefits and the opportunity for profound personal exploration, it also holds the potential for less desirable outcomes if approached without proper care.

One key recommendation for beginners is to approach complex or highly unrealistic activities with caution. Diving into ambitious tasks, such as attempting to fly in your initial lucid dreams, could lead to a sense of disappointment or fear if the experience doesn't unfold as hoped. It's advisable to gradually build up to more fantastical endeavors as you become more adept at navigating and controlling your dream environment.

Additionally, it's important to be mindful of the actions you take within your dream, especially those that deviate significantly from real-world possibilities. Temporarily suspending disbelief is one thing, but engaging in actions with high stakes or extreme outcomes should be reserved until you've honed your lucid dreaming skills. Moreover, try to avoid closing your eyes for extended periods within the dream unless you intend to wake up, as this action is often used as a method to exit the dream state. However, this knowledge can be beneficial if you ever find yourself wishing to leave an uncomfortable lucid dream.

Incorporating known individuals into your lucid dreams can add a layer of complexity to your experience. While it might be tempting to fill your dreams with familiar faces, it's essential to recognize that interactions within dreams do not always reflect real-life relationships. Focusing excessively on particular connections in the dream world could lead to unrealistic expectations or misunderstandings in waking life. If you do choose to involve people you know in your dreams, strive for balance and avoid becoming overly invested in these dream-induced scenarios.

Perhaps most importantly, maintaining a positive mindset is vital for a rewarding lucid dreaming experience. Negative thoughts have the power to shape the dream landscape, potentially leading to distressing or frightening scenarios. Remember, lucid dreaming is an exploration of your subconscious mind's vast terrain, making it susceptible to the influence of your current emotional and mental state. If you're contemplating confronting a fear or exploring a sensitive topic within your dream, proceed with caution and ensure you're in a resilient and positive headspace. Cultivating an atmosphere of positivity and open-mindedness before embarking on your lucid dreaming journey can significantly enhance the quality and enjoyment of your dream experiences, fostering growth and insight rather than distress.

By adhering to these guidelines and approaching lucid dreaming with mindfulness and respect for its power, you can navigate this fascinating state of consciousness in a way that enriches and enhances your waking life.

# CHAPTER 6: ADVANCED TECHNIQUES

Like mastering any skill, lucid dreaming begins with foundational techniques suited for beginners and progresses to more complex strategies reserved for those with experience. This journey into the realm of lucid dreaming is an ongoing exploration, revealing endless possibilities and opportunities for growth. Veterans of lucid dreaming, some with years or even decades of practice, often express the sentiment that they have merely begun to explore the vast potential of what lucid dreaming can unveil. The human mind's boundless nature means that even after a lifetime of lucid dreaming, one could only experience a fraction of the myriad experiences and insights it has to offer. While the prospect of dedicating considerable time to uncover the full spectrum of lucid dreaming's benefits may seem daunting, the rewards it holds for dedicated practitioners are invaluable.

The encouraging aspect of this journey is that as you deepen your acquaintance with your subconscious mind, your repertoire of lucid dreaming capabilities expands significantly. Beyond the initial phase of attaining awareness within your dreams and achieving basic control over dream elements, lies a treasure trove of advanced techniques waiting to be discovered. These techniques not only refine your control over the dream world but also open up new avenues for personal insight, creativity, and emotional healing.

As you progress, you'll find that lucid dreaming is more than just a series of techniques; it's an intimate dialogue with your inner self. The advanced stages of lucid dreaming offer tools for exploring your deepest fears, desires, and aspirations in a safe and controlled environment. This exploration can lead to profound personal growth, enhanced problem-solving abilities, and a richer, more nuanced understanding of your own psyche.

Moreover, as your skills advance, lucid dreaming can become a platform for experimentation and learning. From practicing real-life skills within the dream to resolving complex emotional issues, the possibilities are as diverse as they are profound. The key to unlocking these advanced opportunities lies in patience, practice, and a deepening connection with your subconscious mind.

## Enhancing Lucid Dreaming Skills

Embarking on the journey of lucid dreaming can initially present challenges, including difficulties in manipulating the dream or unexpectedly exiting a thrilling dream due to excessive excitement. The balance between consciousness and the dream state is delicate; our brains construct elaborate inner worlds while providing just enough awareness for us to savor these creations. Yet, intense emotional reactions can disrupt this balance, prematurely ending the dream by catapulting us back into waking life. Similarly, becoming overly fixated on external realities, such as the physical presence of one's body in bed, can destabilize the dream, leading to its dissolution.

Navigating the nuanced spectrum between engaging too little and becoming overly immersed is crucial for sustaining lucid dreaming. This equilibrium is key to preventing the dream from fading or losing its coherence. Establishing techniques for dream stabilization is therefore vital, acting as anchors within the dream to counteract excessive emotional responses or distractions from the external world.

To bolster your lucid dreaming practice and maintain stability within your dreamscapes, consider integrating a more comprehensive set of dream stabilization strategies:

- Detailed Observation: If the dream begins to lose its vividness, concentrate on examining your hands or another specific object. This focused attention can help draw out the details and colors of the dream, reinforcing its stability and clarity.

- Physical Sensation: Rubbing your hands together or engaging in other tactile actions can generate physical sensations within the dream, anchoring you to the lucid state. This tactile feedback loop can serve as a powerful reminder of your presence within the dream.

- Environmental Manipulation: Spinning or performing other movements can act as a reset button for your dream environment. This tactic not only helps in redefining the dream's setting but also in reaffirming your control over the dream narrative.

- Mindful Engagement: Deliberately focusing on the sensory experiences of the dream—its sights, sounds, and textures—enhances your lucidity. This heightened awareness helps solidify your connection to the dream world, making it more resilient to disruptions.

- Verbal Affirmations: Articulating your desires or intentions within the dream, such as seeking greater clarity or lucidity, directly communicates your will to your subconscious, reinforcing your control over the dream.

- Active Movement: Avoid remaining stationary for too long, as this can blur the lines between your dreaming and waking states. Engaging in movement within your dream encourages a dynamic interaction with the dream world, keeping it vibrant and alive.

Incorporating these advanced techniques into your lucid dreaming practice not only stabilizes your dream experiences but also expands your capacity for exploration and creativity within the dream world. As you refine your approach and deepen your understanding of the dream state, you'll discover an ever-widening horizon of possibilities. Lucid dreaming becomes a rich canvas for personal growth, emotional healing, and the exploration of the vast landscapes of your subconscious mind. Through dedicated practice and exploration of these stabilization strategies, lucid dreaming evolves into a profound tool for self-discovery and the realization of your innermost desires and potentials.

## Advanced Lucid Dreaming Techniques

After establishing a foundational understanding of how to anchor your consciousness within a lucid dream and employing basic control methods, it's crucial not to overlook these initial steps. They lay the groundwork for engaging in more sophisticated and powerful lucid dreaming techniques. Mastering the fundamentals of lucid awareness and control is a prerequisite for delving into the realm of advanced strategies that can elevate the lucid dreaming experience to new heights.

As you grow more adept in the art of lucid dreaming, exploring advanced methods of manipulation within your dreams can significantly enhance the depth and richness of your dreamscapes. Among seasoned lucid dreamers, five advanced techniques stand out for their effectiveness:

- Verbal Commands: Just as you might speak to your subconscious to maintain lucidity, directly addressing your dream environment or characters can solidify your influence over the dream. Articulating commands or wishes aloud—such as "Follow me" or "I command that cloud to vanish"—requires a firm belief in your ability to effect change. This conviction is key to actualizing your spoken intentions.

- Object Utilization: Leveraging dream objects or environmental elements can be a powerful method of control. Many adept dreamers create or discover portals for travel or imbue objects with special "powers" to aid in dream manipulation. Whether it's a traditional magic wand or a personal talisman like a unique stone, assigning a specific function to this object—and believing in its power—can facilitate the realization of your desires.

- Physical Gestures: Employing physical actions within the dream can serve as a direct means to influence your surroundings. For aspiring flyers, repeatedly jumping might eventually lead to flight, while others might use hand movements to mimic telekinesis or orchestrate environmental transformations. Such bodily strategies rely on the physical expression of your intent to shape the dream world.

- Emotion Regulation: Gaining mastery over your emotions in a lucid dream can have profound effects on the dream's trajectory. Positive reactions to uncontrollable characters or events—such as embracing a challenging figure—can bring unexpected levels of control. This approach suggests that by accepting and engaging with all facets of your dream self, you foster a more malleable and cooperative dream environment.

- Creative Visualization: Beyond these four strategies lies a broad spectrum of personalized techniques unique to each dreamer. From vividly visualizing desired outcomes to embodying specific characters or qualities, these methods tap into the limitless creativity of the dreamer. For instance, assuming the persona of a character you wish to interact with can invite their presence into your dream.

Exploring these advanced lucid dreaming techniques opens up a world of possibility, allowing dreamers to not only experience the extraordinary but also to engage with the deeper layers of their subconscious. As you refine your skills and venture beyond the basics, lucid dreaming becomes a dynamic canvas for personal exploration, creativity, and transformation. Whether it's through verbal affirmations, imaginative object use, physical cues, emotional mastery, or inventive visualizations, each technique offers a pathway to realizing the full potential of your dream world.

# CONCLUSION

As we draw the curtains on this enlightening journey through "Lucid Dreaming: A Beginner's Guide to Mastering Your Dreams," it's time to reflect on the expansive world we've navigated together. From the initial exploration of the mysteries of sleep and dreams to the practical steps toward becoming an architect of your own dreamscapes, this guide has aimed to equip you with the knowledge and techniques to unlock the boundless potential of your subconscious mind.

We began our adventure by delving into the intricacies of sleep, understanding its phases, and recognizing the crucial stages where lucid dreaming finds its playground. This foundational knowledge set the stage for the exploration of why we dream, offering insights into the theories and potential benefits behind our nightly voyages.

The core of our journey, "How to Lucid Dream," presented you with the initial techniques to awaken within your dreams consciously. Reality checks, dream journals, and mindfulness practices were introduced as tools to bridge the gap between the waking world and the dream world, opening the door to a realm where the impossible becomes possible.

The exploration of "Lucid Dreaming Benefits" revealed how this practice transcends mere curiosity, offering transformative potentials for creative expression, problem-solving, emotional healing, and personal growth. Lucid dreaming emerges not just as a fascinating phenomenon but as a powerful modality for enriching one's life.

"Exploring the Dream World" invited you to take the reins of your lucid dreams, to interact with dream characters, manipulate environments, and control narratives. This chapter aimed to inspire you to embrace the creative and liberating potential of lucid dreaming, encouraging you to experiment and discover the limitless possibilities of your subconscious mind.

Lastly, "Advanced Techniques" pushed the boundaries further, challenging you to refine and deepen your lucid dreaming skills. These sophisticated strategies are designed to enhance your control, stability, and clarity within the dream world, making each lucid dream a more profound and impactful experience.

As you close this book, remember that the journey into lucid dreaming is uniquely personal and infinitely expansive. The practices and insights shared here are just the beginning. Your subconscious mind is a vast and uncharted territory, ripe with opportunities for discovery, growth, and joy. Lucid dreaming offers a unique lens through which to view yourself and the world, providing a canvas for your deepest fears, desires, and aspirations to be understood and transformed.

May this guide serve as a trusted companion on your journey into the depths of your dreams. Here's to countless nights of adventure, exploration, and insight as you master the art of lucid dreaming. The journey is yours to continue, and the dreamscape is your limitless horizon.

Made in the USA
Las Vegas, NV
09 May 2024